Paris
Portraits of France©

Photos Jacques Guillard
Original text Adeline Pron
Translated by Jacqui Taylor

Conception et direction éditoriale Bertrand Dalin

Cover - Wonderful view of place de la Concorde.
Two fountains frame the Luxor obelisk with its hieroglyphic-
covered sides. In the background, the church of La Madeleine.

Previous page - Paris at a glance, from the skyscrapers of La Défense
and the bois de Boulogne on the left to the Sacré Cœur on the right.
The river Seine flows lasciviously through the middle of the busy town.

Summary

Previous page - Imposing Hôtel de ville de Paris, built in Renaissance style by François I in the XVIth century on the site of an earlier building dating from 1357. The Town Hall was destroyed in 1871 during the Commune, then rebuilt on identical lines in 1882 with the proceeds from a national fund.

Paris throbs at the feet of the unchanging Iron Lady.

Editorial

Recalling the City of Light (Ville Lumière) never fails to conjure up a picture or a feeling. For some of us it's the twinkling lights on the Eiffel Tower and our tightly-clutched metro ticket, for others it's small children laughing at a Guignol puppet show, or the story of the fall of the Bastille; munching a 'jambon-beurre' (ham in a baguette sandwich) or the golden glimmer of the pont Alexandre III in the sunshine...

In these pages you'll find the different facets of the capital: Paris the Lover, with its romantic quays and its cosy gardens; Fantastic Paris and its many amusements; Cultural Paris with its plethora of museums and theatres; Liberal Paris, its gay quarter and its cheeky cabarets; Luxurious Paris with its top-class hotels and its 'haute couture' shops. The book sets out to bring together all the types of Parisian ambiance in a single guide.

Let the words and pictures speak for themselves.

Previous page - The wall for Peace, inspired by the Wailing Wall in Jerusalem, bears the inscription of the word 'Peace' in 32 languages.

Hôtel des Invalides, built at the request of Louis XIV to house wounded soldiers. The remains of Napoleon Bonaparte are buried in the church crypt.

History

Around 250 B.C. Paris was only Lucotetia, later shortened to Lutèce (Lutetia) which meant 'shipyard on the river'. Anchored to an island – today the Ile de la Cité – and peopled with a tribe of Celtic fishermen, the Parisii, the little town started to get bigger after 52 B.C. with the Roman conquest.

Some remains of this era still exist, such as the Cluny thermal baths and the Lutèce amphitheatre in the V arrondissement or district. The town was ready to expand when Clovis, king of the Francs made it his capital in 476. Alas! Charlemagne scorned it in favour of Aix-la-Chapelle. Paris did not regain capital status and really begin to rise in importance until the arrival of the Capetians right at the end of the Xth century.

Musée Carnavalet, ' Paris' memory', housed in an elegant XVIth century mansion.

Hôtel de Cluny, abbot's residence built in the XVth century next to the former thermal baths, is a beautiful example of Gothic civil architecture.

The face of today's Paris was already becoming visible in the Middle Ages. The Conciergerie was built next to the royal palace – now the Palais de Justice, or law courts – to house the king's steward. Philippe Auguste had a wall put up with 70 towers in it, two of which can still be seen from the rue des Jardins-Saint-Paul. The Louvre, originally a simple fortress, was built at the end of the XIIth century. It was transformed into a luxurious royal residence under François I's influence.

Arènes de Lutèce in the Vth arrondissement. Built at the end of the I[st] century this amphitheatre was destroyed by barbaric invasions in 280 A.D.

Musée de Cluny, opened in 1844. It houses the remains of medieval Parisian monuments.

Following page - Portes Saint Denis (left) and Saint Martin, triumphant town gateways put up to the glory of Louis XIV's victories.

The business quarter developed on the right bank of the river, while the left bank became the home of the intellectuals: in the Latin Quarter independent colleges were founded, under the Pope's immediate authority, and merged into one single entity, the University of Paris, established in 1215. Religion was the town's other strong point, shown in the construction of Notre Dame Cathedral then the Sainte Chapelle – intended to shelter Christ's crown of thorns – on the Ile de la Cité, seat of royal and episcopal power.

The Middle Ages were also marked by the first political crises in which Paris clashed with the power of the monarch. After the rebellion led by Etienne Marcel, head of the bourgeoisie in the States General of 1355 and 1356, Charles V had the Bastille fortress built, hoping it would discourage future attempts at insurrection.

The Louvre. Magnificent pavilion in the Denon wing with its finely-sculpted façade.

Two centuries later, the Bourbon dynasty arrived on the throne, after the bloody Wars of Religion and the Saint Barthélemy massacre. The future Henri IV, a Protestant, had to convert to Catholicism before Paris would submit. Little by little, during his reign and his descendants', the town became the capital of architectural style, elegance and wit. Salons, philosophy clubs and cafés sprang up everywhere, favouring the exchange of ideas.

The taking of the Bastille, symbol of hostile absolutism, came about after several decades of monarchic excess, as the gap between the people and the aristocracy went on widening. The revolutions of 1830 and 1848 - the first marking the fall of Charles X, the second the return to the Republic – then the Commune insurrection in 1870 were seen as signs of Parisian independence when faced with the ruling power.

The Bastille column commemorates the July revolution of 1830, displaying the names of its victims in gold letters engraved on the bronze.

This didn't stop the nation's leaders working to embellish and extend Paris. Napoleon gave the town monuments that looked like Roman temples, such as the Stock Exchange (la Bourse) and the church of the Madeleine. Majestic monuments like the Arc de Triomphe or the Vendome column celebrate his military successes. Sewers, abattoirs and bridges were opened while drinking water became available for all.

Like an antique temple, the Stock Exchange put up by Brogniart under Napoleon is edged with Corinthian columns.

Following page - The church of the Madeleine was first a military monument. Christened 'Temple of Glory', it commemorated Bonaparte's victories.

In the second half of the nineteenth century, Paris really became the 'City of Light' under the influence of the Prefect of the Seine, Baron Haussmann. Public lighting was now widespread, and the unhealthy old quarters were replaced by long, wide thoroughfares. The landscape gardener Alphand created parks and gardens. There were 1.7 million Parisians in 1852, and the 12 arrondissements had grown to 20 by 1860, with the annexing of the nearest suburbs (Passy, Auteuil, the Batignolles, Montmartre, la Villette, Bercy).

A new type of building appeared, on 5 floors divided into apartments and supplied with lifts. Strongly criticised at the time, Haussmann's Paris is today admired the world over.

Freestone, skylights, corbelled balconies, Haussmann's style is seen everywhere in Paris.

Following page - Fine example of a bourgeois building in the Haussmann style, avenue Camoens.

At the dawn of the XXth century Paris was coming to symbolise parties and pleasure. It was the beginning of the Belle Epoque and bohemia: visiting the Universal Exhibition by day and slumming it in Montmartre by night. The capital hosted five exhibitions in the second half of the XIXth century. It was an opportunity for the nation to show off its artistic and scientific creativity and for Parisians to see the growth of their architectural heritage.

The Eiffel Tower, pont Alexandre III and Grand Palais were flagships of these prestigious exhibitions. 1900 saw the building of the metropolitan. The station entrances were designed by the artist Hector Guimard. Today his work can still be admired at the Abbesses and Porte Dauphine metro stops.

Round the corner, the Eiffel Tower. It seems to be everywhere, watching over the town.

Following page - Pont Alexandre III, sumptuous with its bronze statues and candelabra, golden sheaves and cherubs.

The Great War brutally ended this march of progress. During the inter-war years, architectural development stagnated. In contrast, the arts were in full swing. These were the Roaring Twenties, 'les années folles'. The surrealist poets, Breton, Eluard and others, American writers such as Hemingway and painters like Picasso would meet up in the brasseries of Montparnasse.

Restored building from medieval Paris
in the Marais quarter.

After the Second World War, which saw Paris under Nazi occupation, it was essential to rebuild and also to forget. A certain intellectual frenzy took over Saint-Germain-des-Prés. New literary cafés, the Flore, the Deux Magots attracted Jean-Paul Sartre, Boris Vian and others. Cellars were transformed into dancefloors. The authorities set a vast building programme in motion. Thanks to the Malraux law of 1962 the old quarters were renovated, notably the Marais.

With its almost identical brick and stone houses, its arcades and garden greenery the Place des Vosges is a huge cloister right in the heart of Paris.

The first RER suburban train line arrived, opening up the suburbs confining families of modest means and immigrant communities. Of course the centre of Paris remained the stamping ground of the upper middle class. In May 1968 the social and political crisis affecting the nation reached its height, in the Latin Quarter in particular, where students clashed with police. The city was showing the strength of its revolutionary temperament once again.

Urban development took on a new direction under President Georges Pompidou. It was the age of architectural utopias, imagined by De Gaulle and carried out by his successor.

Place de la Sorbonne during a student break.

Following page - Forum des Halles, huge shopping centre under a glass roof, built on the ruins of the wholesale market that fed Paris for 800 years.

Among the most significant examples are Forum des Halles, Beaubourg art centre, Montparnasse tower and La Défense. Like the kings, each president wants to leave his mark on Parisian stone, and to hell with the controversy.

Valéry Giscard d'Estaing rehabilitated the green spaces and transformed the Gare d'Orsay from a station into a museum. He also gave the city municipal status. Jacques Chirac was thus elected first Mayor of Paris in March 1977.

François Mitterand in his turn had great projects carried out: the Bastille Opera, the Grande Arche at La Défense, the Great Louvre, the Bibliothèque Nationale de France. Under Jacques Chirac, the giant sports stadium known as the Stade de France was inaugurated, and new metro and RER lines were opened.

Since 2001, the Mayor of Paris Bertrand Delanoë has endeavoured to rehabilitate the east of Paris. Around the new library and the MK2 complex an urban site of 360 hectares is being constructed.

Bibliothèque François Mitterand, inaugurated in 1995. Successful contemporary architecture from the plans of the architect Dominique Perrault.

Between now and 2015, this quarter should house green spaces, a business centre and a university campus. The architect Jean Nouvel is to deliver a Primitive Arts museum, which will be installed quai Branly.

Also planned are the refurbishing of the La Villette basin and the transformation of the former XIX century undertakers into a cultural centre devoted to the performance arts. Under the same impetus, the Gaieté lyric theatre (III arrondissement) closed for 15 years will reopen converted into a centre for numeric arts and current music.

Paris stretches out towards infinity, is modernised or rises from its ashes, offering the visitor a face with a variety of expressions, each one merry and attractive. Paris will always be Paris...

The Géode, cinema with hemispherical projection, part of the ambitious and futuristic cultural complex La Villette.

Following double-page - Esplanade du Louvre, a vast open space in the heart of Paris. The glass pyramid crowns the Louvre palace, renovated and extended between 1981 and 1993 by the architect Pei.

Places

From the top of the Eiffel Tower, reached by means of the original hydraulic lifts, you can take in the whole city – or almost. What heresy to visit Paris without taking this opportunity to measure distances at a glance, identify the monuments – the Sacré Coeur far away, the Trocadéro just in front, Notre Dame over there – and the villages that make up the city, and admire the Seine flowing through the middle. The Eiffel Tower is an ideal starting point for a trip through Paris, and it reflects one of the most beautiful images of the capital.

Previous page - View of the pont Mirabeau.
In the background the Eiffel Tower provides
an astonishing contrast to the American-style
skyscrapers along the waterfront, quai de Grenelle.

Engineer Eiffel's tower was strongly criticised when
it was built in 1889 for the Universal Exhibition.
Today, it symbolises Paris.

Back down to earth. You cross the Champ de Mars, an exercise ground for young soldiers in 1765, later the scene of great revolutionary events and Universal Exhibitions. In the distance is the Hotel des Invalides with its golden dome. This former military hospital put up by Louis XIV now houses the Army Museum and Napoleon's tomb.

Previous page - From the top of the tower, you can take in the whole of Paris – or almost. Here, the Champ de Mars, Ecole Militaire and Montparnasse tower.

Cannons lined up near the Ecole Militaire, founded by Louis XV in 1751 to train 'poor gentlemen' for the military professions. Napoleon Bonaparte was a member of this school in 1784.

A few steps away is the marvellous Rodin museum in the hotel Biron, the XVIIIth century mansion where the sculptor spent the last years of his life. Go for a wander in the gardens and breathe in the scent of lemon trees and roses.

In the Rodin museum gardens, you can gaze at some of the sculptor's famous works.

Summer relaxation in the shady, sweet-smelling park.

Rodin spent the last nine years of his life in the hotel Biron, a magnificent XVIIIth century residence.

It's very pleasant to stroll through Saint-Germain-des-Prés in the afternoon and have a drink on the terrace of the Deux Magots café, opposite the capital's oldest church. There's often a mime artist disguised as a statue to entertain the passers-by. Saint-Germain was an intellectuals' paradise after the Second World War, and is still the quarter for bookshops, publishers and literary cafés.

Previous page - Café de Flore was once popular with artists and intellectuals; Dali, Sartre and Camus were regulars in their time. Today, film stars and their hangers-on like to be seen there.

Restaurant Lapérouse, quai des Grands-Augustins, dating from 1766. Auguste Escoffier, the 'king of cooks' was its chef during the Belle Epoque.

Coming back to the quays, you can stop in at the Musée d'Orsay. This former station built for the Universal Exhibition in 1900 has been used as a theatre and an auction room. Now housing works of art from the period 1848 to 1914, the museum contains an Impressionists gallery where you can admire Monet's Waterlilies and Manet's Déjeuner sur l'herbe.

Institut de France, created in 1795.
The academicians hold solemn
sessions under the mythical cupola.

Following page - Theatre, auction room
and film set: the gare d'Orsay was all these
before becoming a museum in the 1980s.
It houses works of art from the second half
of the XIXth and early XXth centuries.

South of Saint-Germain lies Montparnasse, stamping ground of intellectuals between the wars. Some artists' studios, such as Antoine Bourdelle's, have survived among the rather unattractive modern architecture. The sculptor's home, which contains his works, has recently been enlarged by the architect Portzampac and given a charming garden.

The controversial Montparnasse tower, built in 1969, is 200m high and offers a spectacular view. A few minutes' walk away, close to the rue de la Gaieté with its theatres, sex shops and tourist restaurants, is the peaceful Montparnasse cemetery. Maupassant, Sartre, Balzac and Serge Gainsbourg are buried here, among other national celebrities.

The Montparnasse tower is a steel and smoked glass tube rising to 210 metres. Its panoramic bar offers an exceptional view from the 56th floor. At the foot of the building, a large shopping centre contains restaurants, sports halls and shops.

Montparnasse cemetery, laid out in 1824,
houses the tombs of many artists and writers.
During the first half of the XXth century,
the quarter was known for its painters,
sculptors and intellectuals.

Hanging 18 metres above the railway lines,
stretching over 3.5 hectares, the Jardin
Atlantique is a breath of fresh air in the
heart of Montparnasse.

Leaving Montparnasse, you go along the boulevard de Port-Royal and pass in front of the Val-de Grace hospital, a superb monastic site founded by Anne of Austria. The openwork campanile of the church's Baroque dome pierces the sky; its architect Gabriel Le Duc wanted it to be identical to the one on St Peter's Church in Rome.

Coming back down to the Seine, upriver from the Gare d'Austerlitz, the Bibliothèque François Mitterand rises up before you. Four monumental towers represent open books framing a basement garden, in its turn lined with study rooms. Twelve million works are stored in these austere glass keeps. Launched by François Mitterand in 1988, this vast project was directed by the architect Dominique Perrault and finished in 1996.

Queen Anne of Austria vowed to have a church built if she gave birth to a son. On 6 September 1638 Louis XIV was born; seven years later the first stone of Val-de-Grace church was laid.

Following page - Original structure of the Bibliothèque François Mitterand, calling to mind open books.

A stones' throw away is the bubbly rue Mouffetard that dates from Lutetian times, and hosts a busy market. The houses have kept their XVIIth century sloping roofs and skylights and some even have their painted stone shop sign.

The Pantheon church is the last resting-place of the nation's great men, and was built in the reign of Louis XV. Originally dedicated to Paris' patron saint, Geneviève, this sanctuary was renamed Pantheon in homage to the Roman temple.

From the bottom of rue Soufflot you have an unbeatable view of the monument. Unfortunately there is no way of stepping back to get such a view of the Sorbonne. You have to go into the inside courtyard, then to the amphi-theatres where Dante and Calvin studied, in order to admire this mythic university (which began as a modest college for the poor) as it deserves to be admired.

Previous page - Formerly a church, the Pantheon, finished in 1790, is today the last resting-place of great Frenchmen. Voltaire and Victor Hugo are buried there.

The Sorbonne, originally a modest theology college for penniless students. Now it's the most famous Parisian university.

Lower down is the Ile de la Cité, the cradle of Paris. You'll admire the precious detail on the Gothic façade of Notre Dame. Inside, the archaeological crypt contains Gallo-Roman remains, unearthed in 1969 during the building of an underground car park!

Previous page - The Ile de la Cité, known as the cradle of Paris, welcomes numerous tourists and is the seat of Justice. The police headquarters are on the quai des Orfèvres, made famous in films and thrillers.

Last Judgement portal, sculpted in stone in the XIIIth century, main entrance to Notre Dame Cathedral.

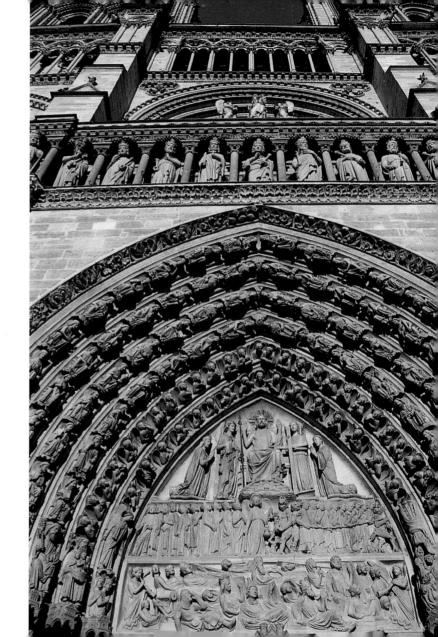

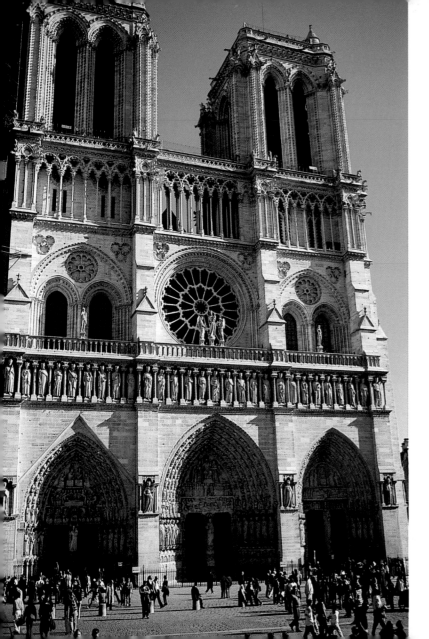

Notre Dame Cathedral is a Gothic masterpiece rising majestically above the Ile de la Cité. It was put up on the site of a Roman temple between 1163 and 1334.

Following page - A clever balance of horizontal and vertical lines supports the cathedral's imposing mass.

Continue the walk to the Sainte-Chapelle, a Gothic architectural treasure founded by Saint Louis. It's considered to be the most beautiful church in Paris, bathed in daylight streaming in through the monumental stained-glass windows.

Just next-door, the Palais de Justice and the Conciergerie used to form the Palais de la Cité, seat of Roman authority then a royal residence until 1358.

During the Reign of Terror that followed the French Revolution, many condemned prisoners, like Marie Antoinette, spent their last hours here.

Sainte-Chapelle, archetype of monumental Gothic art, houses relics of Christ's Passion. Buttresses support the church, maintaining the spread of huge glass panels by means of a solid metal framework. The stained-glass windows are decorative, and close off space like real walls.

Following page - Originally housing the concierge and the guards from the Palais de Justice, the Conciergerie became a prison at the end of the XIV[h] century and remained one until 1914.

The village of Chaillot, annexed to Paris during Haussmann's great public works, is all wide avenues and luxurious mansions. Today the museums are this residential quarter's main attraction. It must be said that the Palais de Chaillot, which is a 1930's neo-classical building, makes a marvellous frame for the Trocadéro gardens and encases the Eiffel Tower like a jewel.

Previous page - A great many strollers come to relax on the Trocadéro lawns in fine weather. The most daring bathe in the gardens' fountain basins.

From the top of the Eiffel Tower, a view of the Trocadéro, Chaillot and in the distance, the tall buildings of La Défense, headquarters of many big companies.

The avenue des Champs-Elysées begins at the place Charles-de-Gaulle or 'Etoile'. Twelve thoroughfares converge here, radiating out like the arms of a star - hence the name.

The Arc de Triomphe, built for Napoléon, overshadows the most beautiful avenue in the world, which used to be simply a place for an afternoon walk. Nowadays the Champs-Elysées host the nations' great events. With its exceptionally fine monuments, the Petit Palais, Grand Palais and pont Alexandre III, this quarter is one of the most sumptuous in Paris.

Arc de Triomphe, most famous Parisian monument after the Eiffel Tower, put up in Napoléon I's reign.

Following page - Baron Haussmann configured the place de l'Etoile, adding seven main roads to the five existing avenues.

At the bottom of the avenue is the place de la Concorde. The architect Gabriel laid out this huge octagonal square in the XVIIIth century, and Louis XVI and Marie Antoinette were guillotined here.

The 3,300–year-old pink obelisk was brought from Luxor by Napoleon I. From here, the rue Royale runs down to the church of the Madeleine, whose height and 52 Corinthian columns give it the look of an antique temple.

Close-up of one of the two fountains in the Concorde, which date from 1840. It took a lot of artists to create these characters, listed historic monuments, as is the whole square.

Following page - Place de la Concorde, the Seas fountain (foreground) and the Rivers fountain surround the Luxor obelisk with its hieroglyphic-covered sides. Add the Madeleine in the background, and this really is a sublime view.

Shopping fans will want to stay a while in this quarter, where there there are plenty of luxury boutiques. In the rue du Faubourg-Saint-Honoré, between the Elysée – the President of the Republic's residence since 1873 – and the British Embassy, you'll find the prestigious names in fashion shoulder-to-shoulder with renowned art dealers.

Previous page - The National Assembly's antique-style façade matches the Madeleine on the other side of the Seine, just as Napoleon wanted.

TCafé de la Paix, at the foot of the Opéra Garnier, hides some imposing decoration designed by Charles Garnier himself. On the terrace, it's fun to play Hunt the Celebrity.

Vendome column, copied from the Trajan column in Rome, is topped with a statue of Napoleon and commemorates his victory at Austerlitz.

Place Vendome shows off some splendid Louis XIV architecture. It is well known internationally for it jewellers and the prestigious hotel, Le Ritz

Not far off, the elegant place Vendôme is the home of famous jewellers. It was Mansart, the Versailles architect, who dreamed it up. Le Ritz, that luxurious hotel with its posh customers, dates from the late XIXth century.

Several blocks away, you'll find the department stores on boulevard Haussmann; the Printemps and the Galeries Lafayette, which trace their existence back to the Second Empire, close this golden triangle of shopping. At Christmas these temples of consumerism dress up their brightly lit windows with animated scenes to thrill the kids.

La Samaritaine, department store symbol of Art Deco architecture.

The quarter around the Opera is full of cinemas, theatres and brasseries. The famous 'grands boulevards' begin here.

Acrobats, mime artists fire-eaters and musicians put on a show on the piazza opposite the George Pompidou centre.

The bubbly atmosphere continues at the Forum des Halles, a 70 000 square metre underground shopping complex built in 1977. This rather mournful maze replaced the great market of earlier times – 'The belly of Paris' as Zola called it – whose produce had been feeding the capital for over 800 years. Above the Forum, the wide terrace set with gardens, cafés and a remarkable Renaissance fountain, the Fountain of the Innocents, is crowded out at the weekend. The rue Montorgueil runs along the edge of the Halles. In this pedestrian precinct lined with grocers', butchers', bakeries and caterers you'll find the cheeky humour and the cockiness typical of the early XXth century Halles.

Pompidou Centre. This daring example of modern architecture designed by Renzo Piano and Richard Rogers was finished in 1977. It houses the National Museum of Modern Art, a library, two cinemas, theatres and a restaurant.

Following page - Glass pyramids in the peaceful Halles garden, covering a tropical greenhouse.

A short walk away you'll find the Marais, a village within the city, where a mixed bunch of people like to stroll and generally enjoy themselves. Henry IV rehabilitated this unhealthy swamp when he created the place des Vosges. The Marais is full of activity all week, except Saturdays in the Jewish quarter around the rue des Rosiers, and should be visited with curiosity, at a leisurely pace. Apart from the trendy shops and cafés, there are excellent museums like the Musée Picasso and the Musée Carnavalet, which tells the story of Paris, hidden inside private mansions.

Musée Carnavalet, private XVIth century mansion devoted to the history of Paris.

Following page - Place des Vosges, oldest and most beautiful square in Paris. The 36 houses of brick and stone with their slate roofs and bulls'-eye windows make for perfect symmetry.

Coming back to the place de la Concorde you pass the Palais-Royal and the Louvre. The rue de Rivoli, built during the reign of Napoleon I, separates these two former royal residences.

The romantic walks in the Tuileries gardens are lined with lime and chestnut trees. Here and there one of Maillol's statues adds its touch to the landscape.

Following page - At the corner of the rue des Pyramides and the rue de Rivoli Joan of Arc boldly holds up her flag.

Today the Palais-Royal, abandoned by Louis XIV in 1692, houses the Council of State, the Comédie-Française and the Palais-Royal Theatre. There are galleries and antique shops under the arcades.

The garden is quieter than the courtyard, which is visited by a lot of people curious to see the strange striped columns planted there by Daniel Buren.

It was Napoleon who had the Louvre transformed into one of the biggest museums in the world. In the Richelieu wing, the Café Marly offers a superb view of the glass and steel pyramid inaugurated in 1989. Leoh Ming Pei, an american architect, designed this original monument.

Previous page - Once a king's residence, the Palais-Royal now houses the Council of State. Roller-skaters and skateboarders play on the esplanade facing the palace.

Main courtyard. Mobile steel spheres decorate the fountain basins and mirror the palace galleries. Daniel Buren's striped columns are in the background.

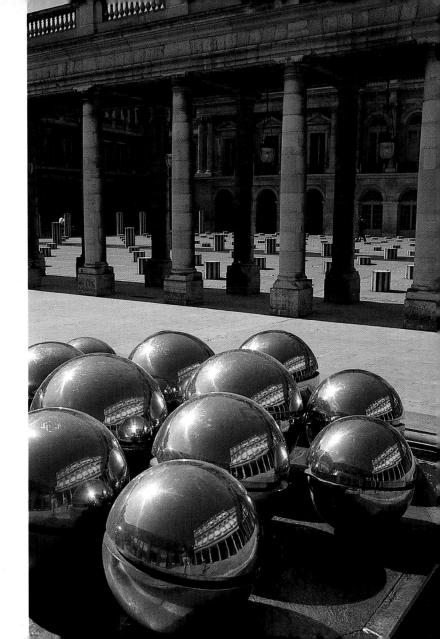

It was on the 'martyrs' mountain', Montmartre's original name, that the first Bishop of Paris, Saint Denis, was tortured in the IIIth century. Montmartre gives you a change of scene, but you can easily feel suffocated. The Sacré-Coeur and the place du Tertre, cute as can be with its cafés and painters, are always overcrowded with visitors.

Previous page - White as alabaster, the imposing Sacré-Coeur Basilica topping Montmartre's hillock looks like theatre scenery.

Place du Tertre, among swarms of people. A stroll, a drink on the terrace – and why not have your portrait drawn?

A survivor of the Belle Epoque, the Lapin Agile cabaret, which counted Apollinaire among its regulars, still attracts custom. At the Abbesses, a pretty little shady square, the Art Nouveau metro entrance in glass and wrought iron has been kept intact.

Lower down, you discover Pigalle and the Moulin-Rouge, once a local hop, today a music hall. This den of iniquity was Toulouse Lautrec's favourite haunt. Pigalle, sex-shop heaven congested with tourist coaches has little in common with the Montmartre of the past.

In the alleyways of Montmartre, the street urchins have gone and tourists have taken their place.

Following page - Those mythical cabarets of the Belle Epoque, the Elysée Montmartre and the Moulin Rouge, still host shows and dances.

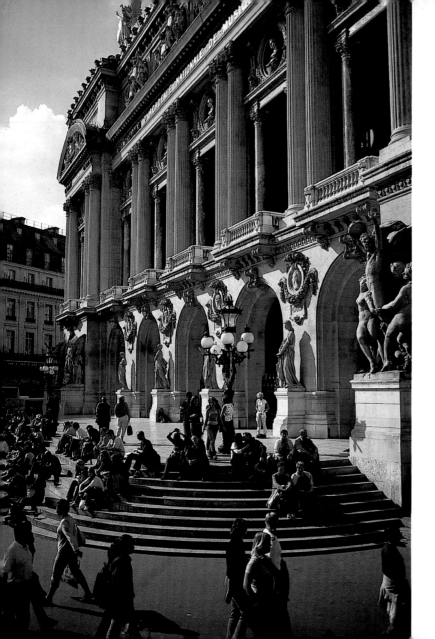

On the 'grands boulevards', synonymous with celebration and pleasure, you'll find many places of entertainment. The expression 'boulevard comedian' comes from here. Between Madeleine and République there are lots of theatres and brasseries, with the occasional building given over to business.

Among the stopping-points along the route are the Olympia, which looks like an American music hall, and the Palais Garnier designed in the Second Empire and mingling Baroque and Classical influences. The façade is richly decorated with friezes, columns, coloured marble and gilding. Further on is the Théâtre des Variétés, scene of Offenbach's triumph, and the Musée Grévin, where famous people have been transformed into wax models.

Steps of the Palais Garnier, ideal meeting-place.

Following page - Opera Garnier, superb building commissioned by Napoleon III, is one of the key places to see in Haussmann's transformation of the capital. It was opened in 1875. The young architect Charles Garnier was unknown when he won the competition held to find a designer.

Nowadays there's a big glass ocean liner on the former site of the Bastille prison. This is the Opéra Bastille, opened in 1989.

Opposite, there's a bronze column known as the 'colonne de Juillet', topped by the Genie of Liberty symbolising the revolutions of 1830 and 1848. All around the Bastille there are narrow streets like the rue de Lappe, known in the 1930s for its 'bals musette' (street dances accompanied by an accordion player), the rue de la Roquette, the rue de Charonne and the rue du Faubourg-Saint-Antoine where wood craftsmen plied their trade from medieval times onward. For several decades these streets have been attracting both artists and night birds of all kinds.

Rue du Faubourg Saint-Antoine, traditionally the wood craftsmen's quarter since the Middle Ages. In 1700 there were 500 joiners and 400 cabinet-makers here.

Following page - If the Opéra Garnier mainly performs ballets, the Opéra Bastille, created in 1992, was designed for lyric art.

To the east, Belleville on its hill, together with its hamlet Menilmontant, are all the rage. Belleville's steep alleyways and colourful markets are a refuge for many immigrants who live cheerfully side-by-side in this ethnic melting pot.

Père-Lachaise, which links the villages of Belleville, Menilmontant and Charonne, is the biggest, the greenest and the most picturesque of cemeteries.

The romantic paths, little woods, statues and here and there, unusual mausoleums in this marvellous garden reflect the XIXth century's artistic variety.

Colette, Jim Morrison, Haussmann, Chopin, Molière, Piaf and Proust, among other famous people, are buried here.

Previous page - Far from being a morbid place, Père-Lachaise cemetery, biggest in Paris, is a wonderful garden and a cabinet of architectural curiosities.

The Cité des Sciences et de l'Industrie is a hands-on museum rather like a theme park.

Towards the south, Bercy is a changing quarter. After the opening of a general-purpose sports centre sheathed in grassy lawn on the edge of the Seine and the building of a monumental viaduct to house the Finance Ministry the City of Paris has gone back to traditional ideas by refurbishing the village's former wine warehouses.

The site now hosts the Museum of Fairground Arts and the Bakery School. In the Cour Saint-Emilion, served by the new metro line, arts and crafts shops, a big cinema, wine bars and places of entertainment have appeared in the ancient wine storehouses and gaze at each other across a charming paved precinct.

Cour Saint-Emilion, all the rage for strollers. Arty boutiques, restaurants and bookshops have replaced the wine storehouses.

Following page - The Paris-Bercy general-purpose sports centre (Palais omnisports) is a strange building with walls of glass and grass. Entirely adjustable, the biggest venue in Paris hosts concerts, figure-skating shows, tennis tournaments and even windsurfing competitions!

Directly opposite on the west side of the city, La Défense has been a contemporary quarter with a different style since 1958. This ultramodern, even futuristic site, with its gigantic buildings, serves as an experiment for contemporary architecture and urban development.

La Défense, as the prototype of the modern city, breaks with the picturesque Paris of the past. In 1989 the Grande Arche was put up on François Mitterand's initiative, and the quarter began to attract tourists for the first time. This remarkable monument symbolises Paris to the same extent as the Eiffel Tower or the Arc de Triomphe, being the end point of the 'Triumphal Way,'

that sublime perspective which runs from the Louvre and passes through the place de la Concorde, then the Etoile.

Previous page - 1958 saw the building of the CNIT at La Défense, a real technical feat. Its glass walls and archway are listed historic monuments.

Futuristic skyscrapers of La Défense, Paris' business quarter, calling to mind the towers of Manhattan. Greenery and sculptures – here, Henri de Miller's Sleepwalker – break up the geometrical straight lines.

*Above - Late XIX*th *century bronze statue
to the glory of soldiers who defended Paris,
unusual in this glass and steel universe.*

*Left - Uprights, reflections and shadows:
the towers change their appearance with the
light and the time of day, putting on a live show.*

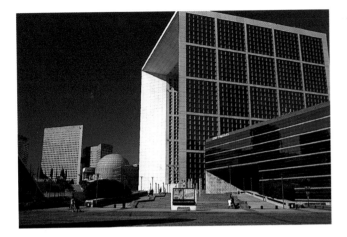

*Grande Arche de la Défense, an empty white
cube with 100m sides. It was built from
the plans of Johan-Otto von Spreckelsen,
and finished in 1989.*

*The empty space under the Grande Arche is
as wide as the Champs Elysées and could
shelter Notre-Dame Cathedral.*

Fresh Air

Although Parisian pollution reaches alarming new heights every year, the city is full of peaceful corners where you can find fresh air. The Seine is lined with pretty, shady quays, strictly forbidden to motorists on Sundays. For the last two years in summer, some of the riverbanks which are not being used for local dances or roller-skaters have become sandy beaches with deck chairs, beach umbrellas, children's animation and even ice-cream sellers!

Previous page - Paris at the beach. Every summer, on the initiative of the Mayor of Paris, some of the capital's quays are covered with soft sand. Deck chairs, palm trees, beach umbrellas and ice-cream sellers put the finishing touches to the illusion.

Discover Paris on a bike, a real pleasure in August or on Sunday morning, when drivers give up the paving stones to the 'petite reine' or two-wheeler.

At street level, the riverbanks have been occupied since the XVIth century by the 'bouquinistes', second-hand booksellers. You'll recognise their famous green stalls or 'boxes', which contain all kind of treasures from rare first editions to old postcards, well worth the rummage from one to the next. The busiest quays are Saint-Michel, Montebello and la Tournelle. On the île Saint-Louis, the quai d'Anjou, built between 1630 and 1647, is without a doubt the capital's most beautiful quay.

Previous page - Pont Saint-Michel, built in 1857
during Haussmann's Parisian renovations.
It replaced a stone bridge put up in 1617,
which in turn followed a succession of wooden
bridges rebuilt each time the Seine flooded,
from the XIIth century onwards. The current bridge
bears the imperial 'N' for Napoleon III.

The bouquinistes' green stalls, or 'boxes'
contain many treasures: rare books, old
magazines, out-of-stock comic strips and posters.

To go from the right to the left bank, you cross one of the city's 36 bridges. The pont Alexandre III represents the Art Deco style in vogue during the third Republic, and is without doubt the most sumptuous. The exuberant decoration – gilded statues, candelabras and stone lions – was intended to seal the alliance between Russia and France.

Near the Institut de France, the pont des Arts is a pretty pedestrian walkway full of artists. It was put up at the beginning of the nineteenth century, as a toll bridge for the upper classes. In 1982 it was entirely rebuilt following a different model: the iron was replaced by steel, there are fewer ornamental shrubs and only five arches instead of eight.

Pleasant open space at the foot of the XIXth century Town Hall, transformed into an outdoor skating-rink in winter. Below, the road running along the riverbank is pedestrian on summer Sundays.

Following page - Paris at night. What could be more wonderful?

As for the Pont-Neuf that crosses the Ile de la Cité, it's the oldest and most popular bridge, despite its name. It was opened by Henri IV in 1607, and has practically never been altered.

The great Parisian gardens, mostly laid out in the XVIIth century, used to be palatial ornaments. The architectural style of the residence was thus also reflected in the surrounding park. Green spaces were enclosed in strict geometrical shapes, perfectly illustrating the dictates of the period, when the force of reason absolutely had to triumph over nature.

Pont-Neuf, oldest bridge in Paris despite its name. In 1607, this was the first bridge to be built with pavements and without houses along both sides!

Catherine de Medicis had the Tuileries palace built, but its park became a 'jardin à la française' (French-style garden) under the aegis of André le Nôtre in 1666. The two huge terraces which make up the park are separated by a long, wide walk going beyond the boundary of the residence. The park has been open to the public since the XVIIIth century, and it attracts plenty of visitors, come for the kiosks, the cafés, the stone benches and the chairs placed at their disposal.

Children float wooden ships in the fountain basins of the jardin des Tuileries, as they did in bygone days.

Moments of sunny relaxation in the Palais-Royal gardens, watching Nikki de Saint Phalle's unexpected statues dancing.

The parc Monceau, guarded by its monumental railings, is surrounded by richly-decorated mansions. When it was laid out in 1787, in a manner both frivolous and sophisticated, it was nicknamed the 'Folie de Chartres' (Chartres' Folly) The irregular landscaping in an Anglo-Chinese style calls to mind an exhibition of curios, as its founder Carmontelle hoped it would. Apart from the colourful but classic flowerbeds and the graceful statues, you find an Egyptian tomb, a stalactite-filled grotto and a pool edged with Corinthian columns. The park looks rather like an operetta stage-scene, and is popular with Japanese brides and grooms.

Parc Monceau, laid out in the XVIIIth century, houses several curios, like this Corinthian column.

Following page - The park has hardly changed since its beginnings. Its many statues make for a charming stroll.

A haven of peace in the middle of the teeming Latin Quarter, the jardin du Luxembourg is the place Parisians like best. The palace overlooking them was Marie de Medicis' former residence, and now houses the Senate and a museum hosting important art exhibitions. Photographic exhibitions also take place here; the photographs are displayed on the railings around the park and renewed every six months. Yann Arthus Bertrand's work was the first to be 'stuck up' in this new way during summer 2000.

Previous page - Jardins du Luxembourg, favourite Parisian park. The gardens have everything you could want: tennis courts, a bandstand, chairs to sit down on, splendid XIXth century statues and a puppet theatre.

Palais du Luxembourg, built for Marie de Medicis. Today it houses the French Senate and hosts important art exhibitions.

Inside the park the kids are spoilt for choice: pony rides, a puppet theatre, a playground, and even beekeeping classes! A hive containing more than 20 colonies was installed there in 1856 and is still going. Grown-ups can sunbathe round the ornamental pools, play tennis, or relax by the pretty bandstand . The 25-hectares park was laid out in 1617 by Boyeau de la Bareaudière, the first French garden theorist, and has been reorganised a good many times. There are 80 statues, most of them dating from the XIXth century, and three fountains. The most famous of them was built in the Baroque style in memory of Marie de Medicis, and looks rather like an Italian grotto.

Series of beautiful gardens decorated with statues and lined with chestnut trees down the middle of avenue de l'Observatoire, a stone's throw from the Luxembourg.

The jardin des Plantes was laid out in the interests of science by Louis XIII's doctors. It was originally used to grow medicinal herbs and to house the exotic species brought back from foreign expeditions. Today, some 10,000 varieties of plant are found here.

Among the interesting things to see, you mustn't miss the first cedar imported from the Lebanon and planted in 1734 by Jussieu, the alpine, iris and rose gardens and the oldest tree in Paris, a locust tree or false acacia planted in 1601! The jardin des Plantes also has several species of animal in its menagerie, which dates from 1794 and is the oldest zoo in the world.

Today a place for a quiet walk, the Jardin des plantes médicinales was laid out in 1626 for the king, and opened to the public in 1640. It houses around 10,000 varieties, all carefully labelled.

The 865-hectare bois de Boulogne provides a real breath of fresh air for solitary night birds, joggers and weekend townies missing the countryside. The lawns are great for picnics and the lakes for a romantic row in a boat. The four gardens – Bagatelle, Pré Catelan, Shakespeare and the serres (greenhouses) d'Auteuil – the paths for walkers and horse-riders, the sports facilities and restaurants all make up the air cells of this green lung.

The park was formerly a royal estate, named in memory of Philippe le Bel's trip to Boulogne-sur-Mer, and the forest was reserved for hunting. Louis XVI opened it to the public, and in the XVIIIth century it became a byword for debauchery. Haussmann's landscape gardener Alphand renovated it during the Second Empire. Two racecourses, Auteuil and Longchamp were added, turning the bois de Boulogne into a fashionable haunt for socialites.

Sophisticated cuisine at la Grande Cascade, posh restaurant in the bois de Boulogne.

The jardin de Bagatelle's most beautiful ornament is its rose garden.

Following page - A rowing boat on a lake – what could be more romantic?

Following page - Château de Bagatelle, or 'Comte d'Artois' Folly', built in only two months to lodge Marie-Antoinette, the count's sister-in-law.

Apart from some wonderful plant collections, the park contains grottos, waterfalls and even a Pavilion of Love.

Its counterpart, the bois de Vincennes – the biggest green space in Paris – on the opposite east side of the city is also a former hunting forest. In the XIXth century it was converted into a military parade ground, and suffered amputation and clearing. Alphand replanted trees, and the site was in its turn given a racecourse in 1863. The zoo was added in 1934 and the Parc floral in 1969. This park contains a space devoted to the Impressionist painters. The flora in the landscapes painted by these artists – sunflowers, wheat, sweet peas, roses, bindweed – make up the Valley of Flowers. In summer, there are music concerts on the site.

Parc floral at Vincennes, famous for its theme gardens and its exhibitions. It displays collections that are unique in the world.

Following page - Summer trip in a rowing boat on the peaceful water of lac Daumesnil, in the bois de Vincennes.

Baron Haussmann was behind the two big Parisian green spaces laid out along the lines of an English park. These parks, designed by Alphand, were known as landscaped gardens.

Amazing but true, the parc des Buttes-Chaumont was built on the site of a former rubbish tip!

Hilly parc des Buttes-Chaumont was laid out from start to finish in 1863 by the landscape gardener Alphand, to rehabilitate an unsanitary quarter.

This very hilly space offers a matchless view of the Sacré-Cœur. In fine weather, you can stretch out on the sloping lawns and enjoy the beauty of this totally artificial site, shaped with blasts of dynamite. The result is impressive: rivers, rocks, grottos, a waterfall, a lake, cliffs and woodland make up this ideal garden, proving that the Second Empire landscape gardeners had genius. Everything is fake but looks natural. Extensive renovation work on the site is planned, to be spread over ten years.

Topping this 30-metre cliff is a viewpoint under a small rotunda, which lets you take in the horizon, and gives you a superb view of the Sacré-Cœur.

South of Montparnasse, the parc Montsouris stands out as the replica of the Buttes-Chaumont. Laid out on what were once quarries, in a quiet and airy quarter, its regular visitors are students from the neighbouring Cité Universitaire campus, and artists. It's said that Hemingway loved to walk there.

Unlike the traditional gardens, the contemporary parks aim to take part in local life, and are amusing to look at, supposedly to attract the younger generation. The parc de la Villette is a 35-hectare garden-town, designed by Bernard Tschumi in 1987. It links the Cité des sciences, the Grande Halle and the Cité de la musique, with a clever mix of walks, leisure activities, shows and contemporary art.

Previous page - Parc Montsouris, built on the site of the old Montrouge quarries, pleasantly relaxing with its hundred-year-old trees, bandstand and sculpture-dotted lawns.

Scary dragon slide in the parc de la Villette.

The parc de Bercy was built on the site of disused wine storehouses, between 1994 and 2000. The site has kept its paved streets and a few railway tracks. The vine plots recall the place's history, and three newly-reconverted warehouses have been preserved. The park is made up of huge lawns and flowerbeds on the theme of the four seasons, and it also has a garden dedicated to Itzhac Rabin, the assassinated Israeli Prime Minister.

Romantic garden in the parc de Bercy, laid out around a canal, playing with the theme of water.

Following page - Parc Georges-Brassens, built on the site of the former place du Marché (market place) and the Vaugirard abattoirs. The belfry has been preserved in the middle of the park, where market produce used to be sold by auction. A second-hand book market popular with bibliophiles is held every weekend under the roofs of the old horse market.

On the left bank, the parc André-Citroën stretches over 13 hectares on the edge of the Seine. The park was designed in 1992 following a competition organised by the Ville de Paris, and is built on the site of the former car factory.

This urban park, embellished by a large fountain and canals, is quite surprising.

A white garden symbolises the city while a black garden, heavily shaded, represents the countryside. Two huge symmetrical greenhouses, dominate the site, one sheltering an orangery, the other a selection of Mediterranean flora. Six serial gardens, each associated with a colour, are separated by small waterfalls. A 'garden on the go', a sort of wild and untidy plain, forms a joyful contrast to the severity of the general layout.

Previous page - Monumental greenhouses in the parc André-Citroën framing a peristyle of 120 jets of water which change their flow without warning, to the great amusement of the kids in summertime.

In the parc André-Citroën, a captive balloon takes you fifty metres up in the air.

Another source of fresh air is the canal Saint-Martin, constructed on the initiative of Napoleon I to supply the city with drinking water. This 4.5 km-waterway extends the canal de l'Ourcq, and was immortalised in Marcel Carné's film *Hôtel du Nord* (1938). Its route is punctuated by locks and swing bridges. You can walk along the banks as if you were on the banks of a Venetian canal. This was once a working-class quarter; today it's one of the most fashionable.

If you like a real change of scene with your walks, follow the 'coulée verte' (greenslide), a path recently laid out several metres from the ground in most places.

It follows the line of the old Bastille-Saint-Maur railway. Original trees and banks of shrubs have been planted on both sides of the walk. For the moment it stops short at the Paris ring road (boulevard périphérique), but there is a plan to go on as far as the bois de Vincennes, as did the earlier railway line.

Covered in parts, the picturesque canal Saint-Martin is 4.5 km long, starting at La Villette and finishing its journey in the Arsenal basin.

Gastronomy

It is usually said that Paris is the Mecca of gastronomy. Yet who can name a regional speciality, or a dish typical of the place?

There are a few vines planted here and there (at Bercy, Montmartre, Belleville and the Clos des Morillons). There are the thick and tasty slices of Poilâne bread, the Paris-Brest cake, shaped like a bicycle wheel in praise of a cycle race, the Parisian, famous ham-and-butter baguette sandwich and the Opéra, biscuit gâteau with almonds, coffee and chocolate invented by the house of Dalloyau, the 72 flavours of Berthillon ice-cream, made on the île Saint-Louis since 1954, and the rare beef still found around the former abattoirs at la Villette.

Previous page - Unrestricted view of the Seine, the île de la Cité and Notre-Dame from the mythical XVIth century La Tour d'Argent, *flagship of French restaurants.*

Paris is also the city of the bar snack.
Break for a ham-and-butter sandwich,
also called a 'Paris beurre', at the Roi du Café.

Paris, however, has no real soil. The provincials, proud of their culinary heritage and their agriculture, are already laughing up their sleeves, thinking that here, they can get their own back on the arrogant big city. Paris hasn't got its own gastronomic culture, they say, and the products tasted and bought there come from elsewhere and are not at all the real thing.

True, but that is the capital's chief asset. The wealth of good food in Paris lies in its diversity, its quality and the number of products, shops selling them and restaurants offering them on their menus.

Breton crêperies abound round Montparnasse. Japanese sushi restaurants are now as common as bakeries. You can find an Italian on almost every street corner. All types of cuisine, international and regional, are served here – and served well. For the desire to do as well as in the place of origin, or even better, motivates both chefs and shopkeepers. We are in Paris, the City of Light, where mediocrity is just not allowed.

Previous page - The best regional products in the capital. At the Comptoir Corrézien, *a grocery with all the charm of bygone days, mellow tiling and painted wooden façade, Chantal cheerfully supplies the best tables in Paris with foie gras and fresh mushrooms.*

Beaumarchais bakery, with its old-fashioned décor, illustrating French craftsmanship and know-how. You'll find the famous traditional baguette as well as an extraordinary variety of special breads.

Every French region and almost every country is represented in Paris.

The Auvergnats, who came to work here in the XIXth century, bringing coal in their luggage, took over the faubourg Saint-Antoine, where you can still taste black pudding with chestnuts, aligot (a combination of mashed potato and Auvergne cheese) and other very filling dishes.

Today, the temples of Parisian gastronomy, rivals in invention and perfection, attract the world's gourmets. The surroundings, the view, the welcome and the discretion of the personnel count for a lot, more so than elsewhere, no doubt.

Opened in 1686 by the Italian Procopio,
Le Procope was the first of the capital's
coffee-houses. It is also the oldest literary café.

Following page - Gastronomic cuisine in
sumptuous XVIII surroundings at the hotel
Meurice, luxury and sophistication guaranteed.

La Tour d'Argent, which dates from the XVIth century, is one of the flagships among great restaurants. The wide picture windows of the first-floor dining room give a plunging view over the île de la Cité and Notre-Dame. There are so many other prestigious places, like *Le Grand Véfour* at Palais-Royal, *Ledoyen* on the Champs-Elysées and *l'Ambroisie,* place des Vosges, to name but three.

The name of the restaurant is however less important to remember than the name of the chef who presides over its destiny and works hard every year to keep the mythical 'three stars' given it by that gastronomic bible the Guide Michelin. Chefs such as Alain Passard (*l'Arpège*), Alain Senderens (*Lucas Carton*) Guy Savoy and Alain Ducasse are almost as famous as film stars.

Opposite and following page - Le Grand Véfour is one of the best French tables, in Directoire-style surroundings, overlooking the jardins du Palais-Royal. An unforgettable moment. Bonaparte, Victor Hugo, Colette and Malraux ate in this historic establishment, which was originally called the Café de Chartres.

Opposite and above – At Le Dôme,
*Montparnasse brasserie opened in 1923,
the chef Franck Graux gives you a glimpse of
today's freshly caught fish. Once a temple of
Roaring Twenties artistic and literary bohemia,*
Le Dôme *specialises in sea produce – fish,
seafood and shellfish, all perfectly prepared.
You enjoy your meal in wonderfully preserved
Art Deco surroundings, while portraits of
pre-war celebrities look down on you.*

In nearly every season you can enjoy oysters, grilled fish and bouillabaisse (Marseilles fish stew) in Paris. One of the best bouillabaisses is served at *Le Dôme* in Montparnasse. Jacques le Divellec, native of La Rochelle, whose restaurant *Le Divellec*, near the Invalides, is the undisputed master of this kind of cuisine. He is nicknamed 'the ambassador of the sea'.

The brasseries are also typically Parisian. They go back to the post-war period of 1870 when the Alsatians were forced to leave their region, and many set themselves up in Paris. This kind of restaurant often specialises in Alsatian choucroute washed down with beer, or seafood, and offers a menu of regional dishes, carefully prepared and filling. The décor is always the same: Art Deco mirrors, stained glass, and imitation leather banquettes. These brasseries punctuate the main avenues at strategic points, often near theatres and concert halls. They are well kept, and considered almost as institutions.

The Grand Colbert, *typical well-kept Parisian brasserie for after the show. Good plain French cooking on the menu, a busy dining room and attentive service, in surroundings that feature mosaic patterns, chandeliers, mirrors and brass.*

The most famous are *Lipp* at Saint-Germain-des-Prés, *Bofinger* at the Bastille, the Lorraine in the Ternes quarter, *Le Vaudeville* at the Bourse and the *Grand Colbert*, towards the Palais Royal.

Yet the Parisians' favourite haunt is still the bistrot, where the traditionally home-cooked dishes are written up in chalk on a slate and served in a warm and friendly atmosphere. The cellars are usually well supplied and you can often order wine by the glass. The Ami Louis in the third arrondissement is a real old-style bistrot. No special care is given to the decoration, and the tables are covered with rough red-and-white checked tablecloths. Here, the ambience and good food prevail.

Original 1900's décor, listed historic monument in itself, at Lipp, *the famous brasserie on the boulevard Saint-Germain.*

Following page.
Left - Café Louis-Philippe *serving regional cuisine and wines on the quai de l'Hôtel de ville.*

Right - At the Restaurant du Marché, *rue Dantzig, the chef Francis Lévèque reinterprets traditional home-cooking with talent. The genuine bistrot décor makes for a convivial atmosphere.*

The big luxury grocers' such as *Fauchon* and *Hédiard,* which face each other across the place de la Madeleine, offer their customers variety, quality and exotica. During the festive season, the two establishments compete for the most original window-dressing, the one with the most spectacular and elegant decoration coming out on top.

Hédiard was founded in 1854, and specialised in importing colonial produce right from the beginning. The stalls overflowed with coloured spices, delicate grains and rare fruit.

Auguste Fauchon was born in 1856 and started life selling fruit and veg at the Madeleine. His shop has been world-famous since the 1930's; you can get cherries or apricots at any season, unusual jams and a whole lot of other exquisite foodstuffs.

Hédiard, *flagship of luxury grocers', has an international reputation. Founded in 1854, it specialised straight away in colonial produce, selling fruit, vegetables, oils and spices from all countries.*

In the middle of the afternoon, what could be more pleasant than a tea break in a salon de thé? Everyone has heard of Ladurée's famous macaroons (rue Royale) and Angelina's mythical montblanc, or chestnut cream dessert (rue de Rivoli). A new generation of pastry-cooks, innovative show-offs like Pierre Hermé, the Parisiennes' new darling, has come along to shake up and wake up these rather outdated places.

Macaroons from Ladurée's patisserie.
With their many pastel shades delicately displayed in a gold-edged green cardboard box, they are as exquisite to look at as to taste!

Gentlemen prefer le zinc, the counter of a little local bar, to relax after the office. The working day often finishes as it started: at the bar, with the morning 'express' coffee making way for a half-pint of lager in the afternoon, or a glass of well-chilled muscadet. The regulars chat to strangers passing through, putting the world to rights, and moan about or commend the latest government measures, according to their views.

Paris is a political capital, and important projects are often thought up and discussed around a table, famous or not.

Café de l'Epoque. *Whether philosophical, artistic, literary or political, the Parisian cafés are part of the historic and cultural heritage of the city.*

Following page - Bar du Marché, *in the heart of the Latin Quarter. Tourists and students from the Sorbonne alike appreciate this café.*